The Art of Leading a High-performing Team

By Sajid Inayat

TABLE OF CONTENT

Overview/Introduction

To simplify the term, the duty of a team leader includes supporting, and guiding a group to actualize a particular result that wished to be accomplished, and supervising the methods that will be employed to achieve those results. It is also the core duty of a team leader to evaluate how the tasks are being implemented. How the leader works, the flow, and the nature of working with the group are dependent on the situation. The leader may sometimes make important suggestions, work in a direct role, concerning what the team should, as well as how they should do it.

The above begs the question, on what does a leader do? A Leader, in collaboration with his team designs, plans, supervises, and implementation a task. These activities can happen either in an implicit, explicit, and systematic manner or in an unfolding and organic nature. The determinant is the need and nature of the team involved.

An excellent team leader begins his or her planning by having a clear picture of what is to be achieved. A question like: "what exactly am I supervising?" will give more information on the planning.

When a leader is skilled, he or she is going to have a quick positive effect on the dynamics of the team. Such leaders helps to readjust any group behavior or stubborn patterns. They help their team members to remain focused and present, which helps their emotional intelligence, as well as help them to fully concentrate on what is at hand.

Effective team leaders allow some time to reflect, and or alternative approach before an action is carried out. They may also unfold some of the faceless assumptions of the team. In most situations, their interventions are usually geared at optimizing the collective capability, as well as knowledge of their team members, in a bid to moving them forward.

This approach is what frees up the team members, and help them delve into some important and critical discussions. A leader will equally ensure that the voice of everyone on his team is heard, and also make sure that the group processing is working. Putting in place such atmosphere is what inspires people to raise concerns, discuss controversial or difficult issues, and come together to find a sustainable solution. At the end of the day, the result is worth it-- a successful outcome, geared in the appropriate path by an organized and cohesive group.

Therefore, a team leader is a changer driver. He or she is someone, whose primary aim is to spark fresh thinking/idea, re-energize the group, and also help his or her team members generate possible solutions to a problem or problems that seem unsolvable.

If you would like to be an effective team leader, this book will help you navigate the intricacies, and maze that you might encounter in becoming a great team leader. Optimizing the productivity of your team can be what you need to hit on to your actualize your goals. Continue with this book, to find out how.

Making Your Team Become Great

There is a proverb that summarizes the fact that, if you would like to go far, you should go together with people, but if you just want to go fast, go alone. It is a fact that for a team to be great, it starts with the leader because he or she will be the one to set the standard.

I will be touching on powerful habits you will need to inculcate for you to inspire your team to greatness.

1. **Don't resist the talent of your team member:** Allow your team members to use their talent. Great leaders allow their team member to express their talents. If you try to prevent that, it will lead to compliance. On the other hand, if you allow for autonomy, you will be on your way to unfolding greatness in your team.

2. **Allow them to make mistakes**: You must make your team know that failing is allowed. Creating a great team requires failing than being timid. Failure is part of the developmental process, which has the capacity to turn your team into what you have always dream of.

3. **Make them work together to achieve a set vision**: The beginning of success and progress for any team is to work on a single vision. If they are able to work together, it is a sign that they will be successful in whatever is being worked at. Things will fall in place if each member of the team comes together.

4. **Demonstrate the quality of a leader, and mentor the leaders within your team:** When you are a leader, you will notice that your habit reflects on your team. It is therefore advisable to demonstrate effective leadership skill and also lead by example. You have to ensure that what you say is in line with what you do. You can then mentor your team member to step into their leadership role. Allow your team members to participate in a leadership role, by encouraging and empowering them.

5. **Equip your team with what they need to become a success:** Of course, there are ways you could find out what your team needs to be successful. Although, you may not be in the capacity to give them everything required, but you can make sure you work hard to give them what they want. For you to know what they really want, just ask them.

6. **Make the atmosphere enjoyable and fun:** A lot of us are able to perform when we are more relaxed and having a nice time. Difficult tasks and overwhelming deadlines are surmounted with fun. Great leaders know how to combine these two elements in their team, without compromising the excellent work ethics or commitment of the team.

7. **Teach them responsibility and accountability:** It is important that you are a kind of leader people can trust with whatever he or she says, and can also trust. You have to develop a solid reputation for being true to your word to become a great leader. What that reflects is that others can count on you, and make them know the kind of behavior to expect

from you.

8. **Be a purposeful and decisive leader:** You have to make decisions, constantly. A team that is doing well with great leaders, knows the importance of being purposeful and decisive. Success and growths rely on predetermined actions, but trying to attain perfectionism will slow things. You have to acquire the confidence to stand alone, as a leader. Include the compassion to listen to the needs of your team members. Also, having the courage to make though decision is one of the cores of great leaders.

9. **The power of emotional intelligence shouldn't be underrated:** Just like IQ, EQ is also important, although, it can be difficult to understand. If you are incapable of having an effective relation or empathy, if you can't manage your distressing emotions, if your self-awareness is poor, or your emotional ability is weak, then regardless of your level of smartness, you won't go far in leading your team.

10. **Make your team know that things are hard, before becoming easy:** You must orientate your team that, nothing comes easy; that they have to work for it. Encourage them to always persist until they get what they want. Let them know that if they are not pushed to the edge, they may never realize their potentials or know their limits. You have to be able to push your team member to the edge. You are teaching them to always go further. They will realize that there is no limit to what they can do if you can constantly push them beyond their limits.

11. **Show them something to grow on and learn from:** Just like the best leaders and teams are never stagnant, you have to create several avenues for your team members to grow and learn from. It can be in form of lunchtime seminars, group readings, classes, or conferences.

12. **Demonstrate bravery and encourage them to be fearless:** An effective leader will encourage his or her team to be great, as well as show fearlessness, take chances, and go out on a limb. As an effective leader, you have to be able to teach, coach and show that you are there with their team. Not just standing at the sideline, instilling fear and screaming at other team members, but encouraging and showing

fearlessness within them.

13. **You have to earn their respect, and let them have yours:** If you want to be a great leader, you need to give your team reasons to respect you. You must equally also respect them. Mutual respect needs to be the norm of a team. You, therefore, need to set an example by treating every of your team member as well as people you meet with respect.

14. **It is important to admit that you don't have all the answers:** You have to be transparent. It puts your human side to play. Your team members should know that being a leader is not about feigning to have all the answers. You should rather focus on leading your team to greatness, by making them see the importance of solving problems collaboratively.

15. **Always strike a win-win situation:** The biggest victory you could make as a leader is not trashing out others, but striking a win-win solution in situations. With this, everyone gets to win, in one way or the other. You have also succeeded in creating more opportunities, that will benefit everyone.

16. **Be flexible and agile:** Effective leaders embrace flexibility, and agility because they understand that things change, and if a leader wants to be successful, he or she must learn to be flexible. When you are flexible and agile, your team will become more cooperative, collaborative, as well as empower them to uphold these qualities.

17. **Build personal and professional relationships:** A great leader builds a personal relationship with his or her team members. Although, it might not be a very close relationship, but to see every member of the team, just beyond a team member, whose job is just to get a task done. Spend some time with them, and get to know them personally. Demonstrate that you have their best interest at heart and that you care about them. By so doing, you have successfully gathered a team, that is ready to unveil their greatness.

18. **Encourage candor and be honest:** You need to be honest and encourage your team member to speak with candor and be transparent, even if things go wrong. Your team needs to have the feeling that they can speak honestly. Speaking honestly about problems, lead to finding sustainable solutions to problems. Like it is said, honesty is the best policy.

19. **Be available and accessible**: You have to be there for your team, as a leader. Peradventure they need your advice or need to question you, you have to make yourself very accessible. Your office should be always open, Check your mails, and your mobile line should be active. What matters most is that your team members can get across to you when they want to.

20. **Always appreciate your team, and praise them often:** Having a great team involves acknowledge and praising them. If you make your team aware that you are aware of their potential, and what they have achieved, you will start benefiting from your team's greatness.

Resolving Conflict in Your Team

It is a common fact that conflict is part of life, as well as our day-to-day interactions. Conflict is unavoidable when you spend time with the same set of people every day. You, therefore, need to create time for conflict resolution, as a leader.

There are different reasons conflicts happen in the workplace, which automatically makes it part of life for managers. In many organizations, part of the work description of a manager is to bring together people with different attitudes, personalities, skills, and ask them to work as one.

This is one of the reasons it is very rare for team tasks to go seamlessly. Even in straightforward and simple ones, conflicts sometimes occur.

The reason is mostly as a result of miscommunications, little disagreement about work, ego or personality clash, and misunderstanding.

You, therefore, as a great leader, need to be responsible to manage your team's conflicts and mediate between the team members involved. Note that there are times when the resentment between your team member, who are at loggerheads, will be difficult for anyone to resolve, let alone you. You just have to come to terms with the fact that some of these conflicts can't be resolved, despite your effort. Be okay with that.

It is important that you don't side with anyone when trying to resolve conflict. Your duty as a team leader is to ensure that the conflicting team members are able to work together on a task, as much as possible, or develop an alternative way to make them more productive if they can't at all work together.

If there is constructive conflict, it can unite a team more, if handled appropriately. Appreciating, respecting, and recognizing the differences of your team member is important in building an effective and strong team. When you resolve conflicts proficiently and quickly, it helps develop a healthy and strong team.

Conflicts can get in the way of team members' productivity and creativity if not handled properly. Here are some of the way you can handle team conflicts:

1. **Recognize the conflict:** It might save you in the short-run if you ignore the issue but note that these conflicting team members will have to work together again, in a future project. The resentment will explode if the unresolved issues are there. This can lead to unpleasant arguments and fights.

Face the conflict head-on, and avoid making the anger build-up. Encourage your team member to speak their mind to themselves, as soon as when the conflict ensues. Although it may not be pleasant, an open expression of this disagreement can help wave off bigger issues.

It is also possible for conflict to bring out the worst in us. Therefore, one of the most important things to note in resolving team conflict is basic respect and civility. Ensure that no destructive behavior is entertained, such as insults, backbiting, insult throwing, setting ultimatum, and insult throwing.

2. **Make your position clear:** Give each member of your team the chance to voice out their opinions, and listen to them attentively. Pay attention to them while they talk, ask questions for clarification, and don't jump into conclusion.

Allow the conflicting members to elucidate and explain their stance. This helps to resolve the problem of miscommunication. Also if you can allow the team member to rationalize their opinion, it can bring about mutual understanding and agreement from the team members.

3. **Jot down assumptions and facts based on each position:** After allowing the conflicting team members to put forward their case, jot down their assumptions and facts.

Just the act of jotting down the rough edges of an argument, and seeing it on paper to check the information with other members can reduce the weight of what seems to be a complicated problem, and make it appear clearer to the team.

If there is no logical reason in the stance of a member of the team, you will see it clearly, using this step. In some cases, team members just want to have their hesitations discussed and heard by other members of the team.

When you are able to analyze the reason for the conflict, as a group, you will be able to find a middle ground to agree on.

4. **Separate the existing alliance and divide into smaller groups:** It is normal for friendship to develop in the place of work. Although this is very good for engaging employees, productivity, and happiness generally. But when it concerns conflict, it can influence the judgments of the team member in determining the appropriate action to take.

There is a tendency that co-workers agree with themselves, because of the fear of losing a friendship. As a leader, you have to break up this alliance during resolution discussion. You can prevent these behaviors, and allow each of the team members to see the conflict the way it is, without the influence of their friend, either explicit or implicit.

5. **Bring the group together:** If these steps have been followed to the letter, it will become easier for the team to meet again as a whole. Having allowed a small group to discuss their issues freely, without the persuasion of their friends, it is common for point of view to change that will unravel a solution for the initial conflict.

After agreeing on a final resolution with your team, write down feasible steps that will be effective in resolving issues. When the solution is written down on paper, it serves as a reference for those, who wish to have a look at the decision of the conflict.

6. **As a team, you may consider celebrating the resolution:** After resolving the conflict, go ahead and acknowledge the contribution of other members of the team. This is what will breed cohesiveness in the team, and make them feel good for working together towards finding a solution.

The celebration can be in form of an afternoon off or a congratulatory email. The point is that; celebrating this middle ground agreed upon will make your team bond better. You have to make this practice the norm in your team, such that they know they will reap the reward of taking a wise approach to solving their conflicts.

As long as it is dealt with quickly and constructively, conflict can be constructive. When you respect the difference between conflicting people and also managing the conflict when it ensues, you will maintain a creative and healthy team atmosphere. As a leader, you have to be open to the idea of your team members, assumptions, and beliefs.

Choosing Your Decision-Making Style

Whenever you are about to make any decision, your decision-making style reflects. According to a study at Columbia University, we all make at least 70 conscious decisions every day, and it doesn't even count into our normal daily routine. There is also another estimate that puts it roughly around 35,000.

You are probably not surprised about this as a leader. There are lots of decisions you will have to make. It can be deciding to resolve conflict at your workplace, or trying to determine which projects should be given more priority, or trying to figure out the best candidate for your HR department. It goes on and on.

What you do when you encounter these choices are what determines your decision-making style. Do you trust your instinct? Do you fall back and gather many opinions before you make your decision? Or are you one of those that throws a dart at a board? There is no single way to arrive at a conclusion. Your style of decision will most likely be different from the decision style of other managers. It is the way you process situations that enables you to make choices.

Importance of Recognizing Your Style of Decision

It is beneficial to know your decision-making style. Here are some:

- **It increases your confidence:** This is essential, knowing that a lot of leaders feel less confident leading their team members. You will have confidence in your decisions if you know how you arrive at that decision.

- **Know your blind spot:** if you are aware of your decision-making style, you will be able to address your weakness before it causes a problem.

- **It enables you to effectively collaborate:** It is good identifying your style, but it is great when you understand how other people arrive at their decisions. You will find group work easier, and delegate tasks efficiently, with information in your hand.

If all these are combined, you will have a clearer picture of why you should understand your decision-making style.

Types of Decision-Making Styles

There is nothing as good or bad when it concerns decision-making styles in the field of management.

With each of the decision-making style having its pros and cons, there are four styles of decision-making styles.

1. **Analytical decision-making style:** Those in this category don't usually make fast decisions. You need to weigh your possibilities, check your facts before you finally decide if this is your style.

Putting together as much information as possible before making your decision, will be your priority if you fall into this category. Although, it consumes a lot of time, but you will feel confident that you have made the best choice based on the information available to you. You will do well with data as an analytical decision-maker. You tend to gravitate towards a person that knows the exact number of information. This might may also be known as integrative or consultative decision-making style.

Recognizing analytical decision-maker

- Most of the time, you take your time to decide on the situation, knowing that the best decisions take time. The time makes you feel confident about your decision.
- You believe that you need enough information to make the best decision. You have it in mind that the more information you have, the better your decision.

- For you, a creative way of solving your problem is fun. You hardly recognize a black or white answer.

Analytical decision-making is best when:

- Some situations need information and perspective from different sources.
- Some situations can be more than one appropriate answer, so you can employ creativity to getting the best solution.

It can be difficult when:

- You need to make a quick decision, and no luxury of time to gather enough information.
- You don't have much information. In this situation, you will have to rely on your instinct over-analysis.

2. **Direct decision-making style:** You have probably heard the word "directive." How does it sound? Like someone is giving commands. This is a good way of having a picture of what this decision-making style is all about.

You will rely on your experience and instinct if you are a directive-decision maker. As a directive-decision maker, you usually don't see the need to gather perspectives or opinions from others before you make your decisions. What people in this category do mostly is to check the pros and cons of the situation, then make a choice. These are people who mostly take charge of a group. These people are sure of what they want, and they will direct people to ensure they get it.

They are also known as autocratic decision-makers or independent decision-makers.

You are a directive decision-maker if:

- You will like to take action. You are always frustrated when people are withdrawn from taking decisions.
- When you take your decisions alone, you have a feeling of

fulfillment.
- You use past results, procedures, and rules to make your future decisions
- People refer to you as level-headed and logical.

This decision-making style is best for:

- Situations that require fast decisions, with no time for agreeing on a consensus.
- Situations when there is a single way forward, or one answer, as seen in previous events, processes, and rules.

Directive decision making can be difficult when:

- There is a need to put together opinions in making decisions, as against being given a directive from the top.
- Going about situations that you haven't experienced before, because there is no template or experience to borrow from.

3. Conceptual decision-making: If decision making seems seamless for you, then this is you. If you are in this category, then you are capable of quickly thinking outside the box, and developing innovative solutions. In your decision-making style, you encourage your team member to think without bonds and pay emphasis on collaboration.

You focus more on the future, as a conceptual decision-maker. What this means is that you not only look at the immediate impact of your decision, you also have your eye on the future impact. People in this category are tagged the idea person in a team. Such people are very inspiring and creative.

They are also called theoretical decision-makers, or visionary decision-makers, or holistic decision-makers.

Knowing conceptual decision-maker:

- You like open-ended problems and questions, which make you thrive with ambiguity.

- People usually tell you that you have great ideas and that you are creative.
- The big picture is always on your mind, as against just reviewing the choices on the table.

This decision style is good for:

- Situations when you have different uncertainties and not a single defined expectation.
- Situation when you don't need to rush into giving answers, quick results, and also having the time to experiment.

This decision style can be difficult when:

- There is a lot of opportunities to try and error, which makes you want to naturally gravitate towards the safest option.
- You have a limited time, that prevents you from considering the big picture, and first pay attention to a short-term solution.
- Your team members are scared of taking risks, as well as the potential for failure.

4. **Behavioral decision-making:** For those in this category, they value the feelings and reactions of people before making decisions. But they don't usually admit it.

When they are about to make decisions, they consider people's needs and emotions. And such people value their relationships. For them, if a decision does not benefit everyone, then they won't bother making it.

As such, the positive reaction of their team is paramount, which means that they seek advice and gather reactions from people before making their final decision.

Behavioral decision-maker, when in a team environment are like the force that makes everyone keep working together. They are also called consensus decision-makers, or relationship decision-makers, or team decision-makers, or flexible decision-makers.

Knowing behavioral decision-maker:

- The togetherness of your team is what is paramount for you. This explains the reason you don't usually make radical decisions.
- You consult widely before making your decisions.
- Your most important asset in the workplace is relationships.

This decision-making style is good for:

- Situations that won't sprout into disagreement or conflict
- Situations when you don't have a popular decision, that can make you go for the most agreeable or popular solution.

This decision style can be difficult when:

- You can't make a popular decision, which makes disapproval and conflicts unavoidable.
- Your focus is togetherness, that makes it override out of the box or creative thinking.

How to Reach a Consensus

Decision making can sometimes be challenging and complex. If you can do it rightly, you will create a smart solution to a problem, and if done poorly, it can have a negative effect on your reputation. However, irrespective of how decision-making can be, it is one of the ways of making a decision.

You will need a team when your decisions involve a large amount of data when different ideas are required, and sampling of different perspectives.

When it concerns making a team-based decision, is there a better way you can manage your team, and make sure that the decision is in everyone's interest?

What to Consider in Team Decision-Making

There are always many perspectives and skills in team-based decisions. The best approach to managing these differences include taking note of these factors:

- **Availability:** The number of resources and time that can be allotted to handle the decision.

- **Decision type:** Does the decision have anything to do with performance, and are they strategic in nature? Is this related to the way things are done in the company? Will the outcome affect the team?

- **Commitment:** Is the team committed to delivering?

- **The kind of task:** Does the team have the required expertise and appropriate knowledge?

Ensuring Team Consensus

After considering the above factors, you will have to align with your team and agree on a decision.

We look at the few tips you can employ to ensuring that every single member of your team feels valued and have a say in decision making. It will easier for team members to find a compromise, that will bring about a final decision.

1. Encourage and ensure participation

Have you witnessed a meeting where a member of the team presents his idea assertively than the others? Often, this leads to a skewed conclusion, that is capable of having a not so good effect on other members of the team.

To avoid this from happening, you may consider introducing the Stepladder Technique when having a team discussion.

This technique requires that all the team members individually think about the problem, then the leader will call each team member, one after the other, and ask for their opinions or ideas. This technique will have all the team members feel acknowledged and heard. It also prevents the ideas of others not to be influenced by others around them, which makes each member confident about his or her opinion, which may not have been possible in a group environment, where there are different ideas.

2. **Consider multi-voting**

Having experienced company meetings and elections, we are familiar with this process. When there are several options, voting is a viable option. But the question is what will happen if all options get an equal amount of vote? It means you don't have a final decision.

However, multi-voting is the solution to such a situation. How is this done? All the members of the team will be giving a specific number of votes with varying weights. After that, each of them will be asked to go through the options and give weight to each of the solutions.

Team members will be able to think through the available options clearly, and using weighted votes reduces the chance of stalemate.

3. **Point out priorities**

Naturally, we can prioritize our tasks, but when we are in a group environment, it can be difficult to collectively prioritize everyone's tasks.

One of the biggest problems encountered by all managers is thinking that a task should be prioritized above others, therefore, how can a resolution be reached? The Modified Borda Count comes handy, in this kind of situation. It helps to create a framework in helping to create priorities, and as well, help a team to decide the option they will preferably place above others.

4. Engage the whole team in developing a solution

It can be hard to make a popular decision when you are working with people with a different point of view and personalities, in a complex project where the solution is not clear.

By using the Hartnett's consensus-oriented Decision-Making Model, it enables all the members of the team to contribute to developing a solution, giving them a sense of ownership in making the final decision, increasing their creativity and ability to think creatively, without the fear of any judgment.

You may consider using the consensus method if there is a problem that needs to be solved and involve team involvement. While this is time-consuming, the benefits are great. It creates an atmosphere of equality among those making the decision. That is, everyone is given a chance to speak, which helps you make a very effective decision, agreed to by the team, coupled with proper implementation because of the commitment and consensus arrived by the team.

Practicing Empathy

One of the keys to healthy relationships in a workplace is understanding people's emotions. It helps to develop a more productive team, improve our quality of relationships with others, and resolve conflicts.

Many people are comfortable learning new skills, but it sometimes seems difficult, learning interpersonal skills. Without minding the feelings of other people, a lot of people are self-conscious when it concerns discussing their feelings.

Oftentimes, we confuse empathy with sympathy, but they are not the same. Plainly put, sympathy is a feeling of concern for people, with the feeling that makes you think that they could be happier. Sympathy doesn't entail sharing emotions or perspective.

So what is empathy? It is the ability to see emotions in others, as well as understanding the perspective of others on a situation. When you are able to develop your empathy, you will be able to use that insight to improve people's moods, as well as support them when going through a challenging situation.

Daniel Goleman, a psychologist defines empathy as one of the 5 most components of emotional intelligence. He stated that empathy develops through three stages, which are:

- Cognitive empathy
- Emotional empathy
- Compassionate empathy

Cognitive Empathy

It can be used by a salesperson to measure the feelings or mood of a customer, allowing them to know what tone to use in communicating with them. Cognitive empathy is also useful for managers to understand how their team member is feeling, making them adjust their leadership style, or what leadership style to use.

Cognitive empathy is the ability to understand what is going through the mind of others, or what they are feeling. It doesn't involve any emotional engagement by the observer.

Most times, cognitive empathy involves emotional, intellectual, and rational ability. It, therefore, goes without saying that it is sometimes used for negative purposes. A good example of this is when a person with a Machiavellian personality trait takes advantage of someone who is emotionally vulnerable.

Emotional Empathy

This kind of empathy can be overwhelming for some people. It can be damaging to people's emotional well-being when those with strong emphatic tendencies become immersed in the pain or problem of others.

When you are able to understand the emotions or feelings of others, then you have emotional empathy. This is what makes you understand someone on a deeper level. It is also known as affective empathy, simply because it changes or affects you. It is not just about understanding people's emotions and feelings. It is also about establishing a sincere conversation with them.

By taking some breaks, you can prevent this emotional burnout. Reinforcing your ability to cope and redefining your boundaries, is one of the ways to withdraw from this demanding role.

If you are a leader, you will benefit from some emotional empathy. Trust is established between team members and managers when there is emotional empathy. But when combined with action, emotional empathy is very valuable.

Compassionate Empathy

This kind of empathy is the most active form. Not only does this compassionate empathy share in this emotion or feelings of others, but it also entails taking some practical steps in making the situation at hand better.

For instance, let say your friend is angry that the presentation he delivered at work was poor. Recognizing that he feels pained and showing the signs of those feelings, is known as compassionate empathy. But in all, setting aside some time, and helping with practical solutions to making sure they perform better in case of next time seals this kind of empathy.

Developing Empathy at Work

It is possible to be scared about committing oneself emotionally, and sometimes even struggle to show empathy, because you feel incapable of doing so. However, that doesn't automatically mean that you are condemned to fail.

You have to put aside your point of view, and see things from other people's angles for you to be able to use empathy effectively. This enables you to see behaviors that come across as unreasonable, stubborn, or over-emotional, as just a reaction that is based on the initial knowledge of a person and their experience.

You will have to practice these techniques often for you to become used to them.

Your full attention is needed

Pay attention to what the other person is trying to tell you. Your body language should be employed for this. Use your instinct, eyes, ears to understand what the other person is communicating.

As you listen, start by noting the phrases and keywords they use, especially if it is used multiple times. Then, think about what is being said and how it is being said. Also, pay attention to their body language. What is it communicating to you? For example, are they scared? Are they ashamed? Are they angry? Note all these before giving your response.

You can go further with this stage, by not arguing, disputing facts, or asking direct questions. Furthermore, note that the direction of the conversation can change, so be flexible.

Note the perspective of other people

"Before you criticize anyone, try walking in their shoes." We have at one point or the other heard this saying. Maintain an open-mind, and examine your attitude. If you focus too much on your beliefs and assumption, it will be almost impossible to be emphatic.

When you can see what other people see, you should acknowledge it. Although, this doesn't mean you should agree with them. However, that moment is not the time for debate, but make sure you listen and respect them.

Ask the person to describe their position, if you are in doubt. Further, ask the reason they feel the issue can be resolved. You need to ask the right question, in the most direct and simplest way possible for the other person to understand.

Act

Showing compassionate empathy doesn't have a template. The dominant emotion at that time, individual, and situation is the sole determinant. Note that it is not about what the other person needs and wants, it is not about what you want. This means that whatever action you take has to be beneficial to them.

Let's take for instance your colleague at work is not able to focus at work, because their child is battling with drug addiction. You can be magnanimous, and ask him to work from home to enable them to keep an eye on their child. But on the other hand, coming to work can be the respite they need to keep their mind away from the problem. It will therefore be better to ask them the approach they want.

Observing the world from diverse perspectives is something interesting. Note that empathy is not just employed when a problem occurs. It can be used in any situation-- all the time. As you must have known, a random act of kindness is capable of brightening anyone's day.

For instance, you are being empathetic if you smile, while trying to remember someone's name. Also, you are being empathetic when you give constructive feedback, curious about people's interests and lives, giving people full attention in a meeting, and so on.

Note and practice these skills, and you will have the reputation of being approachable, trustworthy, and caring, which will be an added advantage to your organization and team. Once you have to open yourself to what other people think, you can feel their experience.

Active Listening Skill

We are in a world driven by technology, where more than ever, communication is important. As much as we communicate, it is worthy of note that we don't listen effectively. Attentive and genuine listening is rare. When we practice active listening, it can help develop, relationship, ensure understanding, solve problems, and help avoid conflict. Your workplace productivity, ability to negotiate, lead a team, and persuade will increase if you practice active listening.

What is active listening? It entails full concentration, understanding, response, and remembering what is being said. This is when you make a deliberate effort to understand the complete message, as against passive hearing.

Importance of listening

One of the most fundamental components of communication is listening. Listening doesn't just happen. We have to make a conscious effort to make it happen.

Listening actively also requires patience because interrupting the speaker with comments or questions will disrupt the flow of understanding. It involves allowing the other person to explore their feelings and thoughts, which you have to create time for.

We spend most of our time listening

Many studies emphasize the importance of listening, as relating to communication skills. On the average, in our waking hour, a study recorded that we spend at least 70 to 80   percent of our time communicating in one way or the other. We spend 9 percent of that time writing, 45 percent listening, 30 percent speaking, and 16 of that time writing.

Research also records that a lot of us are inefficient and poor listeners. A study shows that we only recall 50 percent of what is being said. That is, a lot of us are not a good listener.

The reason we should practice active listening

The benefit of active listening includes:

- **Useful for solving and detecting problem:** You should always be attentive to what your employees say, as a leader. They are always the first set of people to identify flaws in the workplace. And they are likely to come up with solutions or suggestions. You will know and understand what is needed to be adjusted for improvement if you listen to your colleagues.

- **Money and time are saved:** In addition to reducing mistakes and misunderstanding, which could have a negative effect on a business, it could help save money and time, such that you won't have to start a task over again, as a result of not listening properly. There is a budget allocated to a project, and employers won't want to waste resources.

- **Increase knowledge and competence:** Effective listening skill increases your capability, competence, irrespective of your position. If you can listen actively in a meeting, the more information you will get that will help you in completing a task successfully. You can also build your knowledge base with listening, which can aid you in life long learning.

- **You will become approachable:** People will be gravitated towards listening to you if you appear to be a patient listener. You will give people the freedom to express themselves when you are there to listen attentively to them.

- **Your patience is strengthened:** For you to become a great listener, you have to develop it over time. It takes consistency and patience to develop. However, as you gradually improve at it, an additional benefit is it develops your patience. This is when you allow other people to express themselves freely and honestly, without being judged.

- **Your perspective is broadened:** Your perspective of this life is not the complete perspective of the world. One way of looking at life is through your perspective. When you listen to other people's perspectives, you will be able to see life from another angle, which you may not have seen if you don't listen to people.

- **Trust is deepened:** When you listen sincerely, people will want to open up to you. They will always have the feeling that you won't jump into conclusion, based on the little details they provide. They will also have the feeling that the reason why you are listening attentively to them is because you care about them. Although it takes time to build trust, but some of its benefits are a promise of help during difficult times, and lifelong friendships.

How to Know You are a Good Listener

If you are an active listener, you will try to understand what others are trying to say, irrespective of how fuzzy the message sound. Not only does active listening involves trying to understand the verbal message, but it also entails the interpretation of non-verbal signals, such as physical posture, facial expression, and so on.

With the aid of non-verbal cues, you also need to show the person that you are listening to them. Non-verbal cues such as nodding, eye contact, smiling, and agreeing with some "yeses," will demonstrate that you are truly listening to them. This feedback makes the person comfortable at communicating honestly, openly, and freely with you.

Others know that they have been heard when you practice active listening. They are also encouraged to share their feelings and thoughts freely.

Hearing and Listening

It is worthy of note that hearing is simply the response of the brain to sound. It doesn't necessarily mean that you are listening. Hearing requires no effort, it is automatic. Most of the time, we are surrounded by sounds. For example, we are used to the sound of songs, construction workers, cars, and so on. We hear this sound, we just sometimes choose to ignore.

Hearing is all about:

- Effortless
- Involuntary
- Accidental

On the other hand, listening is focused, purposeful, as against being accidental. It, therefore, requires effort and motivation. At its best, listening should be focused, active, with the purpose of understanding what is being said by the speaker.

Not only does listening include paying attention to the tone of voice, but also how the person uses their body language. Simply said, it means paying attention to both verbal and non-verbal cues of a message. Your ability to become an effective listener is tied to the degree, to which you understand, and perceive the message.

Listening is all about:

- Intentional
- Voluntary
- Focused

Non-verbal and verbal signs of effective listening skills

You know how it feels when talking to someone, and they are not listening to you. It feels horrible. Some tips can be employed for you to let the speaker know that you are actively listening to them, such as making eye contact, nodding, positive body language, and relevant questions.

Non-verbal Cues of Listening Actively

Distraction: An active listener will avoid distractions. Checking the time, for instance, fidgeting, playing with their hair, picking fingernails, or doodling.

Posture: It is a very essential aspect of face-to-face communication. It says a lot about the speaker and the listener. As an attentive listener, you have to lean sideways while sitting, or slightly forward. Some other signs include resting one hand on the other, or a slight slant of the head.

Eye contact: For shy people, eye contact can sometimes be intimidating. It is encouraging and normal for listeners to look at speakers. You have to gauge how you maintain eye contact in all situations. Your eye contact should be accompanied by non-verbal cues, such as a smile, to encourage the person speaking to continue.

Smile: You can show the listener that you are listening to them, just by smiling. It can also be a way of showing them you are agreeing to what is being, or that you are happy about what is being said. Smiling is very powerful in the sense that you are indirectly telling the speaker that you understand what they are saying. You can combine the smiling with nodding.

Verbal cues of Listening Actively

Clarification: In most case, it involves asking open questions, that allows the speaker to elaborate on the points being made. Clarification includes making sure you get the actual and correct message, asking the speaker questions to ensure that you understand the message.

Questioning: Asking some open questions can be employed to demonstrate that you are paying attention to the speaker. When you ask relevant questions, it reflects that you are interested in what is being said.

Recalling: Recall concepts, ideas, and details from your last conversation with the person. It shows that you paid attention to them, which will encourage them to continue speaking with you. Remember some of the key points, such as the name of the speaker for instance. It helps to emphasize that you understand what the person has said.

Positive reinforcement: When you do too much of this, it can be annoying to the speaker. Although this is a strong sign that you are attentively listening. When you occasionally use words like "indeed," "yes" "very good" will show that you are listening.

Four Styles of Listening

The task for public speakers will be easier if listening were easy.

1. **People-centered:** You will be an interesting listener if you are a people-centered speaker because you aim of listening is to learn what the speaker feels and thinks about their message. For Instance, if a people-centered listener is listening to an author of a book, they will be more curious about the personality of the author than the book.

2. **Task or action-oriented:** If your primary concern or interest is what the speaker wants, then you are an action-oriented listener. It is sometimes not easy for an action-oriented listener to listen through the explanations, evidence, and descriptions. Do you want volunteers, donations, votes, or something else? They watch out for the main purpose of the discussion. For instance, you are in a plane, that is about to lift into the air, and the flight attendant gives an instruction saying, "buckle up so we can leave." Buckling up for a task-oriented listener is a compelling message than the reason behind it.

3. **Time:** They can become receptive for a short time, and they can be aggressive and rude when the speaker wants longer attention. A time-oriented listener, like a message that gets to the points very fast. They can be impatient when a discussion is going zigzag.

4. **Content:** They want to listen to well-developed information with

solid explanations. Whether it makes sense, or accurate, or even means anything, content-oriented listeners are interested in the message itself.

Example of active listening

These are examples of the questions and statements employed by an active listener:

- Giving a summary of a group conversation: They give a summary of everything that has been said in a group and confirm with others if what they have said is correct.

- Notice people speaking: They encourage, people who haven't contributed to the topic of discourse at hand to share their opinion.

- Summarize questions: They give a summary, according to their understanding of a question that is unclear.

- Talked about a similar situation: "I have been in such a situation before I left my previous work."

- Asking important questions: "How many people were employed last year."

- Paraphrasing: "So what you are trying to say is that you want to use the template of our proposals for this new project?"

- Short verbal affirmation: "Thank you for the sparing some time speaking to me."

- Asking open-ended questions: "I have been made to understand that you will like a better design. What other features will you like us to add to it?"

Effective Listening Barriers

When a conversation is becoming lengthy, or sometimes, during a brief conversation, we can find it difficult to completely concentrate. Some of the reasons why you fail to be an attentive listener might be something out of your control, while some can be in your control. Being aware of these interfering factors can be helpful. These are some of the barriers to effective listening:

1. **Attention span:** Our attention span is finite. We can only concentrate for a short time. There have been arguments that the audience of nowadays can't sustain their attention when listening to a message. You will find out that when you sometimes concentrate on things that catch your interest, you always pause, and find yourself doing something else, such as replying to a message.

2. **Noise:** Noise is anything that interferes with the ability to understand or attend to a message. One of the biggest factors that interfere with listening is noise. Although, there are different kinds of noise, the ones we mostly encounter are in the situation of public speaking are semantic noise, physiological noise, psychological noise, and physical noise.

3. **Listening Apprehension:** It happens when you have the irrational fear that you won't correctly understand the process or message in question. You can sometimes have the fear that you may not be able to adapt your thinking to coherently adapt to new information. It is also possible that you worry that information will be too difficult for you to understand fully.

4. **Receiver biases:** We all have biases, but an effective speaker avoids falling into them when listening. One of the characteristics of a listener's bias is jumping into a conclusion. It is the belief of a biased listener that they don't have to listen any longer because of what has already been said. Receiver bias includes two things: preconceived opinion or idea about the topic, and biases concerning the speaker. Until the speaker finishes what is being said, a good listener will listen with an open mind.

How to improve active listening skills, and become an effective

listener

Maintain eye contact and face the speaker: Eye contact is considered as essential for effective communication, in the majority of western cultures. We look ourselves in the eye when we talk. Face your conversational partner when you are talking with them. Avoid all kinds of distractions; phones, books, paper, and so on. Even if they are not looking at you, look at them. Although in some circumstances, cultural taboos, uncertainty, shyness, and other emotions, can make eye contact impossible for some people, and you need to understand that.

Be relaxed and attentive: Your undivided attention should be given to the speaker. Note that non-verbal cues are very important. For you to be attentive, you have to:

● Wave off distracting thought
● Focus on what is being said
● Face the speaker
● Maintain eye contact with the speaker

Weed out distractions like noise, and other background activities. Also focusing too much on the speaker's mannerism or accent will distract you from listening effectively. Lastly, avoid being distracted by your own biases, feelings, and thoughts.

Maintain an open-mind: Note that the speaker is using language to represent their feelings, thoughts, going on in their brain. So avoid interrupting until the speaker finishes.
It is important to listen without criticizing what is being said, or judging what is being said. If what is being said alarms you, you can feel alarmed but avoid saying to yourself that "it was a foolish move." You have compromised an effective listening skill if you are already passing judgment.

Avoid cutting them off or interrupting: We use to teach our children that it is disrespectful to interrupt someone while speaking, but unfortunately, we don't seem to adhere to this. Even in TV programs, Talk shows, and all, we find the host interrupting while the other person is speaking.

When you interrupt, these are the messages it sends to the speaker:

- I don't have time for what you have said
- I don't give a damn about what you care
- What I am about to say is more interesting than yours
- I am more important than you

Our rate of thinking and speaker are different: If you are an agile talker and fast thinker, you have to be able to talk slower, for someone who processes slow, and for someone who finds it difficult to express himself or herself.

Clarify what is being said by asking questions: Ask the person talking to clarify his or herself if you don't understand what is being said. Wait till the person finish talking, rather than interrupting. You can say something like. "Can you please clarify this part, where you said..."

Summaries and ask questions to ensure that you understand: Ask questions when the person has finished talking. There are times when we digress from the main point of the discussion, but avoid diverting it to what is not the main focus at hand.

Summarize the conversation to make sure you understand what is being said: This will be very useful to you at networking events because that will give you an excuse to leave the conversation and move to the next person.

Feel the feelings of the speaker: You have to empathize with the speaker. You have to put yourself in the shoes of others to feel empathy. Although, not easy, but not impossible. It takes a huge amount of concentration and energy to achieve. However, that is the right thing to do, because that is what paves way for open communication.

Regular feedback to the speaker: Reflect the speakers feeling, by showing that you know where they are coming from. Occasionally rephrase the messages of the speaker, if what is being said is not clear enough. You can as well show your understand of their message by nodding, or showing appropriate facial expressions, with a well-timed "yea" or "uhm"

Note the non-verbal cues: We can extract enough information from someone just by observing some non-verbal cues. Non-verbal cues reflect in the majority of face-face conversation. There a lot of emotions you could see just by having a face-to-face conversation with people. You could see the slope of the shoulder, how the mouth is set, irritation, boredom, enthusiasm, and so on. All these are cue you shouldn't wave off. Note that non-verbal cues carry more meaning than the words of mouth. Words of mouth are only a small percent of the actual message.

Motivating Your Team

You get important works done because of the input of your team. You can accomplish anything if you combine the knowledge, skills, and energy of motivated people. That said, you can try these approaches to fire up your team to achieve what you aim at.

1. Pay them what they worth

When you are deciding the amount to pay your employee, you have to make sure it is the industry standard. Research has shown that 26 percent of work will leave their current job, just for a 5 percent increase in salary. Don't lose good people to something negotiable.

2. Create an enabling environment for them

We are want to work in a conducive and clean environment. Their work environment can make them feel good. With just a little amount, you can make their working environment conducive.

3. Give them the opportunity to develop themselves

When members of your team get the opportunity to develop or learn a new skill, they will be useful to themselves and the organization. Allow them to attend training that will advance their careers.

4. Promote collaboration in your team

Invite the input of your employees, when you are about to make an important decision. It makes them feel appreciated, and valued. Ask them if there is a better way to do something, and listen to their answers, then apply the solution, if possible.

5. Happiness should be encouraged

Happiness is infectious. Encourage it among your team. Note if your employees are happy with their work or not. If they are not happy, discuss what you can do to make them feel happy.

6. Failure should not be punished

Mistake is sometimes inevitable. No one is perfect. The most important thing about failure is to learn the lesson it offers, for us not to make it again. Don't punish members of your team, when they make mistakes. Just try and encourage them not to feel bad, and try again.

Final Thoughts

No organization will succeed without effective leadership. The primary driver for development and growth in all successful organizations is effective leadership. You must note that being a leader is not about amassing several titles or accolades, it is about being a good team player. It is about having the ability to bring together people of diverse personalities, and background to achieve a common goal. Leadership is something you work for and earn.

Although there is no fixed template for leadership because it depends on the need of an organization and culture. But a good leader will work with his or her team member to increase the productivity of the organization, and also the morale of the people he or she is working with.

More explicitly, being a leader and an effective team player includes being optimistic, inspiring, honest, focus, empathetic, decisive, confident, accountable, and self-aware.

DISCLAIMER:

*The advice provided in this material is general advice only. It has been
prepared without taking into account your objectives, financial situation,
or needs. Before acting on this advice you should consider the
appropriateness of the advice, having regard to your own objectives,
financial situation, and needs. Where quoted, past performance is not
indicative of future performance.*

*The author and the publisher of this book disclaims all and any
guarantees, undertakings warranties, expressed or implied, and shall
not be liable for any loss or damage whatsoever (including human or
computer error, negligent or otherwise, or incidental or consequential
loss or damage) arising out of or in connection with any use or reliance
on the information or advice on this site. The user must accept sole
responsibility associated with the use of this material, irrespective of the
purpose for which such use or results are applied. The information in
this material is no substitute for financial advice.*